IN YOUR OWN WORDS

Volume 1
Sentence Skills

IN YOUR OWN WORDS

A Writing Skills Program for Adults

SEYMOUR GOLDBERG
Assistant Principal, English
New York City School System

JACK NORMAN
Assistant Principal, English
New York City School System

Volume 1
Sentence Skills

CAMBRIDGE
THE ADULT EDUCATION COMPANY
New York • Toronto

Executive Editor: Jerry Long
Contributing Editor: Lisa Wolff
Design: Adele Scheff
Cover: Brian Crede

MANUFACTURED IN THE UNITED STATES OF AMERICA

ISBN 0-8428-9729-1

9 8 7 6 5 4 3 2 1

CONTENTS

TO THE TEACHER

IN YOUR OWN WORDS provides a basic writing program to aid adult students in learning the process of writing. Volume 1 will enable them to write better sentences, to revise and edit sentences, and to perform writing tasks on qualifying tests more effectively.

The book is designed to guide students from basic through sophisticated writing activities. Each chapter presents the following:

- A brief, motivating introduction, culminating in an easy-to-remember summary of the major concepts to be covered in the explanation to come
- A concise explanation of the concept, with clear examples to illustrate each point
- A series of five exercises that become progressively more challenging
- A contextual writing activity that brings together all concepts presented in the chapter and allows students to write an extended passage on their own

The exercises are directly related to adult experience and are thus highly motivating. Students using the exercises will master the skills being taught without being burdened by overly technical explanations. Instead, students will learn primarily through studying the examples and through direct application of the material.

IN YOUR OWN WORDS will help students to increase their knowledge, to challenge their thinking, and to stretch their imagination through writing.

TO THE STUDENT

IN YOUR OWN WORDS will help you to write clear, interesting sentences. Each chapter explains an important concept with clear examples. The five exercises that follow will develop your skills and challenge your thinking. You will learn to write by writing.

By the end of this book, you will be ready to apply your skills to many types of writing. You will be ready to explore in greater detail the pleasures of good written communication.

IN YOUR OWN WORDS

Volume 1
Sentence Skills

PRE-TEST

1 Forming Sentences • Part 1

Begin or end each sentence by completing the thought.

1. My apartment _____.

2. _____ to come with us?

3. _____ cooked a special birthday dinner.

4. Are you _____?

5. Basketball and soccer _____.

2 Forming Sentences • Part 2

Use each simple subject and simple verb in a clear, complete sentence.

6. children   ran

_____

7. brother   plays

_____

8. friends   are driving

_____

9. movie   is

_____

10. we   watched

_____

3 **Sentence Fragments**

Match each sentence fragment in Column A with the best completing part in Column B. Write the letter of the answer on the line.

A	B
_____ 11. When the rain stopped.	a. please answer it.
_____ 12. When summer comes.	b. I helped them with their homework.
_____ 13. If the doorbell rings.	c. we went outside.
_____ 14. After I fed the kids.	d. I was out of work for a month.
_____ 15. Because I broke my leg.	e. we go to the beach.

4 **Run-On Sentences**

Rewrite each run-on sentence as two or more correct sentences.

16. I got up early, I had a lot to do, right after breakfast, I made a list of all my chores.

_____

_____

17. Jack went to the movies did Tina go, too?

_____

18. We went to the park and we had a picnic and then we played ball.

_____

_____

19. I'm tired, let's stay home and watch TV.

_____

20. It's getting late you're going to miss the bus.

_____

5 **Word Replacement**

Rewrite each sentence. Replace the general word with a more specific one.

21. I'm cooking <u>meat</u> for dinner.

_____

22. Your apartment is <u>nice</u>.

_____

23. Mr. Melendez <u>said</u>, "Watch out!"

_____

24. If the weather is <u>bad</u>, we can't go.

_____

25. We went for a ride in Juan's new <u>car</u>.

_____

6 Sentence Expansion

Rewrite each sentence so that it answers the question in parentheses.

26. I'm going to visit my friend. (where)

_____

27. The children went to bed. (when)

_____

28. Maria didn't come with us. (why)

_____

29. I will look for a second job. (when)

_____

30. I parked the car. (where)

_____

7 Sentence Variation

Vary each sentence by changing the order of the words.

31. I like to go ice skating in the winter.

_____

32. At the party, we met Rick and Pauline.

_____

33. The children ate three boxes of raisins during the movie.

_____

34. Because it's getting dark, you shouldn't walk home alone.

_____

35. I was cleaning the apartment when you called.

_____

8 Sentence Combining

Combine these pairs of sentences. You can add, remove, or change the order of words.

36. I bought a coat last winter. The coat is warm.

_____

37. I'm going to the union meeting. Don is going, too.

_____

38. Let's take an umbrella. It might rain.

_____

39. I want to move. Bill doesn't want to move.

_____

40. We had eggs for breakfast. We had toast, too.

_____

9 Sentence Reduction

In each sentence, underline the words that repeat the same thought. Then rewrite the sentence, leaving out the repeated words.

41. My friend Ken, he goes to school at night.

_____

42. Sara uses a tiny, little adding machine at work.

_____

43. We went to the store and bought groceries at the store.

_____

44. Your answer was right and correct.

_____

45. Late at night at eleven P.M., we usually watch the news.

_____

10 The Topic Sentence

Write a complete topic sentence that gives an opinion about each idea.

46. Day Care for Children

_____

47. Getting Along with Neighbors

_____

48. Rules at the Office

_____

49. Family Gatherings

_____

50. Equal Pay for Equal Work

_____

☐ **Check your answers on page 77.**

Pre-Test Evaluation Chart

Use the Answer Key to check your answers. Circle the number of any item you missed. The chart will show you which chapters you may want to spend extra time studying.

Exercise	Item					Chapter
1	1	2	3	4	5	1
2	6	7	8	9	10	2
3	11	12	13	14	15	3
4	16	17	18	19	20	4
5	21	22	23	24	25	5
6	26	27	28	29	30	6
7	31	32	33	34	35	7
8	36	37	38	39	40	8
9	41	42	43	44	45	9
10	46	47	48	49	50	10

CHAPTER 1

Forming Sentences
Part 1

Think about how you learned to talk. First you learned to name things. Then you added information to express yourself fully and clearly. "Ball" became "throw ball," which became a sentence: "I can throw the ball." You learned that to express thoughts clearly, you had to be able to form complete, correct sentences. Complete, correct sentences make your talking and your writing clear.

The major elements in a **sentence** are the **subject** (person, place, or thing) and the **verb** (what is happening to the subject, or what the subject does). The purpose of a sentence is to express a thought clearly.

> ■ **REMEMBER:** A sentence is a group of words, consisting of a complete subject and a complete verb, that expresses a complete thought.

FOCUS ON SENTENCE SKILLS

Any complete sentence has two distinct parts:

1. the naming part, or the **complete subject;**
2. the explaining part, or the **complete verb.**

The train   arrived at the station at seven o'clock.

The sentence above tells about *the train* (complete subject); it explains that the train *arrived at the station at seven o'clock* (complete verb). Together, these two parts form a complete sentence.

In most simple sentences, the complete subject is placed before the complete verb. However, not all sentences follow this naming-explaining pattern. In questions, part of the verb comes before the subject. Contrast the following statement and questions, in which the complete verbs are underlined:

Juan needs a new car.
Does Juan need a new car?
What does Juan need?

Note also the difference in end punctuation. The statement ends in a **period** (.); the questions end in a **question mark** (?).

Some statements can also have part of the complete verb before the subject:

Every summer, my son gets a part-time job.

Statements with more than one thought also follow a different pattern:

Before we went to the movies, we had dinner at a restaurant.

Exclamations indicate surprise or emphasis. They end in a third form of punctuation, the **exclamation point** (!). They can follow several patterns:

We won the game!
Don't touch the poison ivy!
What a great player she is!

There are many different types of sentences. What is needed in every sentence, however, is at least one clear, complete thought.

1 Try Out Your Skills

In each sentence, draw one line below the complete subject. Then draw two lines below the complete verb.

The old, deserted house looked haunted.
Are you going to the movies tonight?

1. The new museum has modern paintings.

2. Seven people were waiting in the rain for the bus.

3. I won $5,000 in the state lottery!

4. Can you come to work earlier tomorrow?

5. Last night we watched a great movie on TV.

6. Do your children like spicy food?

7. In the spring, Maria will join a softball team.

8. My typewriter needs a new ribbon.

9. Have Ken and Yoko found a new apartment yet?

10. Millions of people cross this bridge every day.

☐ **Check your answers on page 78.**

2 Try Out Your Skills

Match each group of words in Column A with a group in Column B to form a clear, complete sentence. Then write your sentences below.

	A	**B**
c	1. Do you	a. we go away on vacation.
___	2. Tom and Kathy	b. coming with us?
___	3. A good résumé	c. like rock music or jazz?
___	4. During the summer	d. wasn't very exciting.
___	5. Are your friends	e. the last person to arrive?
___	6. That movie	f. is difficult to learn.
___	7. Can you	g. decided to get married.
___	8. Am I	h. go camping with you?
___	9. A new language	i. leave work early today?
___	10. Will the children	j. might get you a better job.

1. _____

2. _____

3. _____

4. _____

5. _____

6. _____

7. _____

8. _____

9. _____

10. _____

☐ **Check your answers on page 78.**

3 Use Your Skills

Finish each sentence to form a complete thought. Use correct end punctuation.

> Will you _go dancing with me Saturday night?_

1. The careful driver _____

2. During the fall, _____

3. May I _____

4. My new office _____

5. Tony's interview _____

6. Two weeks ago _____

7. Do your neighbors _____

8. Akiko's apartment _____

9. At three o'clock _____

10. Will your boss _____

☐ **Check your answers on page 78.**

4 Use Your Skills

Begin each sentence to form a complete thought.

The speeding car came to a screeching stop.

1. _____ watch a lot of TV?

2. _____ shook hands with me.

3. _____ are fun to do in winter.

4. _____ have interesting jobs.

5. _____ at the party last night?

6. _____ surprised me.

7. _____ have to keep in good shape.

8. _____ was wonderful!

9. _____ going to join us tonight?

10. _____ is very unusual.

☐ **Check your answers on page 78.**

5 Sum It Up

Complete these sentences about what you learned in Chapter 1. Then check your answers on page 78. If you need more practice, you can re-read the beginning of the chapter and repeat any of the exercises.

A _____ expresses a clear, complete thought. Its main

parts are a _____ _____ (naming part) and a

_____ _____ (explaining part).

In Your Own Words

Write five clear, related sentences about a person you admire. Make sure that each sentence contains a complete subject and a complete verb. Here is how someone might begin:

My neighbor Anita is a very unusual person. She works as a word processor during the day and goes to school five nights a week. At school, she . . .

_____

_____

_____

_____

_____

_____

_____

_____

_____

_____

_____

_____

☐ **A sample is on page 78.**

CHAPTER 2

Forming Sentences
Part 2

Forming sentences is a lot like putting together the pieces of a puzzle. As you learned in Chapter One, the pieces that form a sentence are a complete subject and a complete verb. Now you are going to see how these parts are formed from smaller pieces. The two smaller pieces are a **simple subject** and a **simple verb**.

■ **REMEMBER:** Within each complete subject and complete verb are a simple subject and a simpe verb.

FOCUS ON SENTENCE SKILLS

The simple subject is the key naming word in the complete subject. The simple verb is the key explaining word in the complete verb.

The tired cook   works seven nights a week.

In the sentence above, the complete subject is the tired cook, and the simple subject is cook. The complete verb is works seven nights a week, and the simple verb is works. The simple subject and verb express the basic action of a person, place, or thing. They do not give any added description.

The simple subject or verb can be more than one word:

Dave and Rita work for the same company.

In the sentence above, the simple subject is Dave and Rita.

We have been here before.

The simple verb in the sentence above is have been.

1   Try Out Your Skills

In each sentence, draw a line below the complete subject. Then draw a second line below the simple subject.

> José's new apartment needs a coat of paint.
>
> Does your old car still run well?

1. Our new neighbors moved in yesterday.

2. That red tie looks awful with your yellow shirt!

3. What did the crying child want?

4. My two favorite foods are pizza and chili.

5. Last night my best friend called from California.

6. Barbara's fat cat ate all her plants!

7. The cold, stormy weather kept us indoors all day.

8. A strange letter arrived in the mail this morning.

9. Are the people on this list coming to the party?

10. The long, boring game lasted until midnight.

☐ **Check your answers on page 78.**

2   Try Out Your Skills

In each sentence, draw a line below the complete verb. Then draw a second line below the simple verb.

> I take the train to work every day.
>
> Did you forget your toothbrush?

1. I always walk very quickly.

2. Do you watch the news at night?

3. Mario won the game with his home run.

4. Every weekend Leroy drives a cab.

5. Lisa drove carefully because of the rain.

6. My brother wrote an angry letter to the newspaper.

7. Are both of the children sleeping?

8. Our phone rang late last night.

9. Mrs. Gomez worries about her son.

10. Did you get a raise this year?

☐ **Check your answers on page 78.**

3   Use Your Skills

Use each simple subject and simple verb in a clear, complete sentence. For 1–5, write statements. For 6–10, write questions.

> boy   ran
> The frightened <u>boy</u> <u>ran</u> from the dog.

1. sister   works

_____

2. friends   liked

_____

3. family   is visiting

_____

4. children   watch

_____

5. restaurant   was

_____

6. you   do like

_____

7. son   does want

_____

8. people   did see

_____

9. pitcher   can throw

_____

10. workers   are complaining

_____

☐ **Check your answers on page 78.**

4   Use Your Skills

Match each simple subject in Column A with a simple verb from Column B. Then use the subject and verb in a clear, complete sentence.

	A		**B**
g	**1.** food	**a.**	bored
_____	**2.** movie	**b.**	is
_____	**3.** apartment	**c.**	called
_____	**4.** book	**d.**	seems
_____	**5.** voice	**e.**	bought
_____	**6.** parents	**f.**	like
_____	**7.** friends	**g.**	needs
_____	**8.** children	**h.**	saw
_____	**9.** man	**i.**	played
_____	**10.** team	**j.**	shook

1.   **This Mexican food needs more spice!** _____

2. _____

3. _____

4. _____

5. _____

6. _____

7. _____

8. _____

9. _____

10. _____

☐ **Check your answers on page 78.**

5   Sum It Up

Complete these sentences about what you learned in Chapter 2. Then check your answers on page 78. If you need more practice, you can re-read the beginning of the chapter and repeat any of the exercises.

The _____ naming word in a complete subject is the

_____ subject. Every complete verb contains

a _____ _____. These parts of the subject and

verb contain _____ information, not added description.

In Your Own Words

Write five complete, related sentences about something you like to do in your free time. Then underline the simple subject and verb in each sentence. Here is how someone might begin:

In my free time, I watch sports on TV. . . .

_____

_____

_____

_____

_____

_____

_____

_____

☐ **A sample is on page 78.**

CHAPTER 3

Sentence Fragments

A fragment is a piece of something. Think of a broken vase. Each piece of a broken vase is a fragment of the vase. No piece is complete by itself.

A **sentence fragment** is a group of words that is meant to be a complete sentence. It has the same end punctuation as a sentence, but it does not express a complete thought. To make a sentence fragment a complete sentence, you must join the fragment to another sentence, or you must add to the fragment the part it is missing.

■ **REMEMBER:** A sentence fragment is an incomplete sentence. It may be a long or a short group of words. To make a sentence fragment complete, you must join it to another sentence or add to the fragment the missing part.

FOCUS ON SENTENCE SKILLS

Is the following sentence a complete sentence?

Because it was a cold, windy day.

The sentence has a subject, it, and a verb, was, but it does not express a complete thought. Therefore, it is not a complete sentence. It leaves you with an unanswered question: Because it was a cold, windy day, what happened?

You can complete a sentence fragment in many ways. Here are some ways of completing the example:

Because it was a cold, windy day, we stayed home.

I dressed warmly because it was a cold, windy day.

Notice that when the sentence begins with the fragment, the fragment is followed by a comma. When the sentence ends with the fragment, the fragment comes last, and there is no comma before it.

Here is one goal for completing sentence fragments: The resulting sentence must make sense.

1 Try Out Your Skills

Match each sentence fragment in Column A with a logical completing part in Column B. Then write the complete sentences.

	A		B
d	1. While I was cooking.	a.	I felt much better.
___	2. Although we are good friends.	b.	I must leave without you.
___	3. When the song is over.	c.	they need a lot of attention.
___	4. After I rested.	d.	the doorbell rang.
___	5. When I want to have a picnic.	e.	take a message.
___	6. If you hadn't helped.	f.	I get depressed.
___	7. Every time I watch the news.	g.	I go to the park.
___	8. If the phone rings.	h.	I couldn't have finished on time.
___	9. Because the children are young.	i.	we stopped dancing.
___	10. Since I can't be late.	j.	we often argue.

_____

_____

_____

_____

_____

_____

_____

☐ **Check your answers on page 79.**

2   Try Out Your Skills

Read the following group of sentences. Draw a line below each fragment. The first fragment is already underlined.

<u>When seven o'clock comes.</u> I turn off the alarm and go back to sleep. I would be late for work. If my children didn't shout to wake me up. We all have breakfast together. Unless my oldest daughter is dieting. She is always on a diet. Even though she is already thin. After we finish breakfast. I help the younger children get dressed. Then I get ready for work. Even though some mornings I would rather go back to bed!

☐ **Check your answers on page 79.**

3   Use Your Skills

Change each sentence fragment to a complete sentence. Add words to the beginning or end of the fragment to complete the thought.

> If you aren't busy.
> If you aren't busy, <u>let's get together.</u>

1. Whenever you have time.

   _____

2. After the rain stopped.

   _____

3. When the day ends.

   _____

4. After her husband died.

   _____

5. If you want to help me.

   _____

6. Although the weather doesn't look good.

   _____

7. When the movie ended.

_____

8. Since the office closes at five o'clock.

_____

9. Before the tenants' meeting began.

_____

10. Because it's dark out.

_____

☐ **Check your answers on page 79.**

4 Use Your Skills

Use the following paragraph to form a series of complete, related sentences. Attach each fragment to the words before or after it. Make sure that each sentence makes sense.

When our hopes were almost gone. Our company softball team won the big game. Since we had been the underdogs. We were all overjoyed. Before the game began. We were nervous and unsure of ourselves. Because we had good teamwork. We were able to play better than ever before. Now it was over. And we had won. Although it hadn't always seemed that way. All our hard practice had been worthwhile.

When our hopes were almost gone, our company

softball team won the big game.

_____

_____

_____

_____

_____

_____

_____

_____

_____

_____

☐ **Check your answers on page 79.**

5 Sum It Up

Complete these sentences about what you learned in Chapter 3. Then check your answers on page 79. If you need more practice, you can re-read the beginning of the chapter and repeat any of the exercises.

A sentence fragment is an _____ sentence. To make it

_____, you must _____ a missing part or

_____ the fragment to another _____.

In Your Own Words

Write a series of related sentences using the following fragments in the order given.

1. When the weather on the weekend is terrible.
2. Since we can't go out.
3. If we can't find any chores to do.
4. As dinnertime approaches.
5. If it's still raining.
6. Before we go to bed.
7. If you find interesting things to do indoors.

Here is how someone might begin:

When the weather on the weekend is terrible, we usually have to change our plans.

_____

_____

_____

_____

_____

_____

_____

_____

_____

_____

□ **A sample is on page 79.**

CHAPTER 4

Run-On Sentences

What would happen if this introduction didn't have correct punctuation it certainly would be hard to understand communication with the reader is the main purpose of writing sometimes we make it very difficult for the reader to understand what we are saying.

As you can see, the paragraph above is written as one long, rambling sentence. It needs to be divided into several shorter sentences as follows:

What would happen if this introduction didn't have correct punctuation? It certainly would be hard to understand. Communication with the reader is the main purpose of writing. Sometimes we make it very difficult for the reader to understand what we are saying.

The **run-on sentence** is an error in writing that interferes with effective communication. It must be corrected for writing to make sense.

■ **REMEMBER:** A run-on sentence occurs when two or more sentences are written as one, written without any punctuation at all, written with only a comma, or written with too many ands.

FOCUS ON SENTENCE SKILLS

In a run-on sentence, two or more complete thoughts are improperly combined. A run-on does not have to be long:

Ali left early did Tom leave early, too?

Ali left early. Did Tom leave early, too?

Some run-ons have commas where they should have periods:

> I love music, I have a large record collection, my favorite group is the Rolling Stones.
>
> I love music. I have a large record collection. My favorite group is the Rolling Stones.

Other run-ons have too many thoughts connected with the word and:

> There is a good movie on TV tonight and I want to watch it and then I'll do the dishes.
>
> There is a good movie on TV tonight. I want to watch it. Then I'll do the dishes.

To correct a run-on, identify the complete thoughts. Add a period to the end of each thought. Then begin each new sentence with a capital letter.

1 Try Out Your Skills

Some of the following sentences are run-ons. Write R before each run-on sentence. After the run-on, write the number of sentences it contains.

<u>R</u>   Turn off that light, it's much too bright. <u>2</u>

_____ 1. Our tires are old, we need new ones, we might get into an accident with these. ____

_____ 2. Don't buy a new TV unless you can afford one. ____

_____ 3. The police arrived several hours after we called. ____

_____ 4. This is delicious and I'd like some more and I'd like to get the recipe, too. ____

_____ 5. The game ended in a tie, neither team won. ____

_____ 6. The reckless driver got a speeding ticket it was his third ticket this year. ____

_____ 7. That was a good movie, I'd love to see it again. ____

_____ 8. If you can leave work early, meet me at the station at four o'clock. ____

_____ 9. The phone rang and I answered it and it was Jim. ____

_____ 10. The book was great, but I didn't like the movie. ____

☐ **Check your answers on page 79.**

2 Try Out Your Skills

Read the following run-on sentences. Decide where each new thought begins. Underline the first word of each new thought. The first new thought has been indicated.

My interview was very tiring, it took almost an hour and the manager's assistant tested my typing and I was very nervous and I made some mistakes, I didn't do very well I probably won't get the job but at least I tried my best, I have another interview tomorrow, I really want the job I'll do better after a good night's sleep.

☐ **Check your answers on page 79.**

3 Use Your Skills

Rewrite each run-on sentence as two or more correct sentences.

> Maria left work early, she wasn't feeling well, she decided to go to the doctor.
> Maria left work early. She wasn't feeling well. She decided to go to the doctor.

1. Elena was late they started the meeting without her.

   _____

2. Bill had so much work to do, he had to do the laundry and he had to go shopping and then he had to make dinner.

   _____

   _____

3. Claudia made a mistake, she tried to hide it she got caught.

   _____

4. Julio found a wallet in the street he looked inside it for iden-tification he found a driver's license and some credit cards.

   _____

   _____

5. The children are tired, put them to bed.

   _____

6. We went to the store and first we bought food for the party, then we bought cups and napkins.

_____

_____

7. My son is almost five his birthday is next week.

_____

8. Our union may call a strike I am very worried.

_____

9. We're leaving soon why don't you come with us?

_____

10. Gloria looks sad, she probably didn't get the job.

_____

☐ **Check your answers on page 79.**

4 Use Your Skills

Correct the following run-on sentences by adding some words or by changing some words. This time, do <u>not</u> divide the sentences into shorter ones.

> The sky was growing darker, we brought an umbrella.
> Because the sky was growing darker, we brought an umbrella.

> The concert is selling out fast, buy your ticket soon.
> The concert is selling out fast, so buy your ticket soon.

1. It's getting late, we should leave soon.

_____

2. Call me early in the morning my train leaves at eight o'clock.

_____

3. The prices are getting lower, they're still high.

_____

4. I'd like to see that movie, tell me if you decide to go.

_____

5. It's your birthday I'd like to take you out for dinner.

_____

6. We canceled our trip the car broke down.

_____

7. I'm tired, let's finish the project in the morning.

_____

8. Dress warmly it gets cold here at night.

_____

9. The bus is late, I'll be late for work.

_____

10. Don't give the children candy, it's not good for them.

_____

☐ **Check your answers on page 79.**

5 Sum It Up

Complete these sentences about what you learned in Chapter 4. Then check your answers on page 79. If you need more practice, you can re-read the beginning of the chapter and repeat any of the exercises.

In a _____ sentence, two or more sentences are

_____ together. Some of these sentences have no

_____. Others are joined incorrectly with only

a _____. A third type of _____ error uses too

many _____.

In Your Own Words

This long run-on sentence has no punctuation at all. Rewrite it as a series of correct, related sentences. You may add or take out words where appropriate. Then re-read your sentences to make sure that they make sense and to see that there are no run-ons.

Being a good employee means more than just doing good work it also means having a good work attitude and getting along well with other employees is also very important people must work together they have to respect one another you might not like all your co-workers you must cooperate with them and if you are very unhappy about your job situation you should think it over and perhaps you are not working at a job that is right for you.

Here is how someone might begin:

Being a good employee means more than just doing good work. It also means . . .

_____

_____

_____

_____

_____

_____

_____

_____

_____

☐ **A sample is on pages 79–80.**

CHAPTER 5

Word Replacement

Have you ever listened to someone talking on the telephone? If you have, you probably were bored. In telephone conversations, people repeat themselves using expressions that are general and dull. Some examples of these expressions are "That's nice," "That's great," and "That's too bad." Although you accept such expressions in conversation, you wouldn't want to meet them often in your reading. You also wouldn't want to use them often in your writing.

Your writing should be clear and interesting. It would be both confusing and dull if you used too many general words. Specific words give a clear picture of what you want to say and add interest to your writing. One way to add clarity and interest to your writing is through **word replacement.** As you substitute general words with specific ones, you will see your writing improve. In addition, you will better enjoy writing.

■ **REMEMBER:** In word replacement, general words are replaced by more specific words.

FOCUS ON SENTENCE SKILLS

Compare these sentences:

Anna wore a nice sweater.
Anna wore a warm, colorful sweater.

In this example, a general word, nice, is replaced by more specific words, warm and colorful. The replacement process can be used for action words as well as for descriptive words:

"Nobody understands me," the boy said.
"Nobody understands me," the boy complained.

Naming words also can be replaced:

> That food looks delicious.
> That pasta in cream sauce looks delicious.

Specific time words can replace general ones, too:

> I moved to New York a long time ago.
> I moved to New York seven years ago.

1   Try Out Your Skills

Rewrite each sentence. Replace the general naming word with a more specific one.

> This book is fascinating!
> This novel is fascinating!

1. Those flowers smell wonderful.

   _____

2. Nadia's dog is a good swimmer.

   _____

3. Jack went to the store.

   _____

4. José and Maria bought a car.

   _____

5. Watch out for that insect!

   _____

6. My favorite food is fruit.

   _____

7. Do you like to listen to music?

   _____

8. This soup needs some seasoning.

   _____

9. Do your parents live near the water?

_____

10. Olga's new jewelry is beautiful.

_____

☐ **Check your answers on page 80.**

2 Try Out Your Skills

Rewrite each sentence twice. Each time, replace the general descriptive word with a different, specific descriptive word.

> That was a bad movie.
> **a.** That was a boring movie.
> **b.** That was a silly movie.

1. Steve is a nice person.

   a. _____

   b. _____

2. I'm reading a good book.

   a. _____

   b. _____

3. It's going to be a nice day.

   a. _____

   b. _____

4. The weather is often bad at this time of year.

   a. _____

   b. _____

5. Rochelle's work is always good.

   a. _____

   b. _____

☐ **Check your answers on page 80.**

3   Use Your Skills

Rewrite this story, replacing the general words with more specific ones. Change a to an if necessary.

Last night, I was watching a <u>good</u> movie on TV when the phone rang. It was my old friend, Rita.

"What a <u>nice</u> surprise!" I <u>said</u>. "I haven't heard from you in a <u>long time</u>."

"That's because I moved <u>recently</u>," said Rita. "I got a <u>good</u> job as an <u>office worker</u> in Chicago. I also found a <u>nice</u> apartment outside the city. It has a <u>nice</u> backyard with a garden. Last week, I planted <u>flowers</u> and <u>vegetables</u>!"

"That sounds <u>good</u>!" I <u>said</u>. "I can't wait to visit you!"

Last night, I was watching an <u>exciting</u> movie on TV

when the phone rang.

_____

_____

_____

_____

_____

_____

_____

_____

_____

_____

_____

☐ **Check your answers on page 80.**

4 Use Your Skills

Read these sentences. Underline all the general words that could be replaced by more specific ones. Then rewrite the sentences, replacing the words you underlined.

Last year, Mike and Sue were in a bad car accident. Their car ended up badly. They saved their money for a long time to buy another car. They were happy when they found a used one. It's a few years old, but it's nice. It has a lot of good features, and it's nice to drive. Sue doesn't like the color, though. The car is a light color, and she wants to paint it a dark color.

Last year, Mike and Sue were in a serious car accident.

_____

_____

_____

_____

_____

_____

_____

_____

_____

_____

☐ **Check your answers on page 80.**

5 Sum It Up

Complete these sentences about what you learned in Chapter 5. Then check your answers on page 80. If you need more practice, you can re-read the beginning of the chapter and repeat any of the exercises.

In word replacement, _____ words are replaced by

more _____ ones. If you repeat the same general words

too often, your writing will be _____ and

_____.

In Your Own Words

Write a review of a movie you feel strongly about. Use as many specific words as possible. Write at least five clear, descriptive, related sentences. Do not use the words good, bad, or nice. Here is how someone might begin:

> Star Wars is the fastest-paced, most exciting movie ever made. Its special effects are . . .

_____

_____

_____

_____

_____

_____

_____

_____

☐ **A sample is on page 80.**

CHAPTER 6

Sentence Expansion

Read the following phone conversation:

Caller: Operator! This is an emergency! You've got to send someone over right away!

Operator: Calm down, now. What's the problem?

Caller: I can't explain now. I don't have time! Just send someone over immediately!

Operator: Wait! Don't hang up! Hello? . . . Hello? . . .

Of course, there was nothing the operator could do in this situation. The caller did not give enough information. He or she failed to answer such important questions as *who, what, where, when,* and *why*. These questions are often called the "5W's." They ask for the key information that makes sentences meaningful.

Sentence expansion adds to simple sentences the answers to the 5W's. As you use this method, you will make your writing more accurate and informative.

■ **REMEMBER:** Sentence expansion develops or expands a sentence by answering the 5W's: who, what, where, when, and why.

FOCUS ON SENTENCE SKILLS

To expand a sentence, think of answers to the following questions:

1. Who was involved?
2. What happened?
3. Where did it happen?
4. When did it happen?
5. Why did it happen?

By answering several of the questions above, you can expand upon the information already given in the sentence.

> Maria cleaned the kitchen.
> Maria cleaned the kitchen in her apartment yesterday afternoon because her guests left a mess there.

In the above example, the simple sentence tells only who, Maria, and what, cleaned the kitchen. The expanded sentence also tells where, in her apartment; when, yesterday afternoon; and why, because her guests left a mess there. The simple sentence is correct, but the expanded sentence is more informative and interesting.

Expanded sentences don't have to answer all the 5W's, but they must give more information than simple sentences.

1 Try Out Your Skills

Read each expanded sentence. Then fill out the chart to show which of the 5W's it answers.

1. Marta ate a big breakfast this morning because she was very hungry.
2. Bob wore a clean blue shirt to work.
3. The children are swimming in the school gym.
4. Last night we had dinner at the pizzeria.
5. Dwight struck out eleven batters yesterday.
6. Sue has an interview at eleven o'clock.
7. Kahlil is doing the wash at the laundromat.
8. Tomorrow we're going to the concert in the park.
9. Bill couldn't get tickets for the basketball game.
10. Seventeen people are going to the party at Paula's apartment.

	Sentence Number									
	1	2	3	4	5	6	7	8	9	10
Who	✔									
What	✔									
Where										
When	✔									
Why	✔									

☐ **Check your answers on page 80.**

2 Try Out Your Skills

Each of the sentences in Exercise 1 left at least one question unanswered. Rewrite each sentence, answering one question.

1. **Marta ate a big breakfast at the diner this morning because she was very hungry.**

2. _____

_____

3. _____

_____

4. _____

_____

5. _____

_____

6. _____

_____

7. _____

_____

_____

_____

_____

Check your answers on page 80.

3   Use Your Skills

Rewrite each sentence so that it answers the question in parentheses.

I woke up. (when)
I woke up at seven o'clock this morning.

1. We're taking the bus. (where)

_____

2. Kim left work early. (when)

_____

3. I'd like to take a trip. (when)

_____

4. Carla doesn't want to be a secretary. (why)

_____

5. Frank and Luis went shopping. (where)

_____

6. I hate department stores. (why)

_____

7. My friend just started a new job. (where)

_____

8. We finished all our work. (when)

_____

9. I need some new clothes. (why)

_____

10. Let's have a picnic. (where)

_____

☐ **Check your answers on page 80.**

4 Use Your Skills

Rewrite each sentence so that it answers at least three of the 5W's. (Note: If the subject is a place or a thing, you can say that it answers the <u>who</u> question.) Then write which of the 5W's it answers.

Don worked late.
Don worked late <u>at the plant last night</u>. (who, what, where, when)

1. The children laughed.

_____

2. I decided to move.

_____

3. The game was exciting.

_____

4. Ted invited ten guests.

_____

5. The apartment will be beautiful.

_____

6. We're taking the train.

_____

7. Sam wrote to his brother.

_____

8. I'd like to go out.

_____

9. My friends are visiting.

_____

10. I'm going to take a vacation.

_____

☐ **Check your answers on pages 80–81.**

5 Sum It Up

Complete these sentences about what you learned in Chapter 6. Then check your answers on page 81. If you need more practice, you can re-read the beginning of the chapter and repeat any of the exercises.

Sentence _____ develops a sentence by answering the

5W's: _____, _____, _____,

_____, and _____.

In Your Own Words

If you could have any job for just one day, what would it be? Why? Answer these questions in five or more related sentences. The sentences should answer at least three of the 5W's. Here is how someone might begin:

If I could have any job for just one day, I would be an astronaut.

_____

_____

_____

_____

_____

_____

_____

_____

_____

☐ **A sample is on page 81.**

CHAPTER 7

Sentence Variation

Suppose you lived your life according to a set pattern. Imagine eating the same food, wearing the same clothes, and doing the same things day after day. Life would be very dull!

Your writing would be very dull, too, if all your sentences followed the same pattern. Sentences need variety to be interesting. **Sentence variation** will help you solve the problem of writing sentences that all follow the same pattern.

■ **REMEMBER:** Sentence variation changes the position of words to make sentences more interesting.

FOCUS ON SENTENCE SKILLS

Compare these sentences:

I went to the movies yesterday afternoon.
Yesterday afternoon, I went to the movies.

Both sentences have the same meaning. Only the placement of the words answering the question when was changed. In the first sentence, these words come after the subject. In the second sentence, they come before the subject.

The placement of where and why answers can also vary:

I ran into Tom and Linda in the park.
In the park, I ran into Tom and Linda.

We should take umbrellas because it's raining.
Because it's raining, we should take umbrellas.

Notice that when a group of <u>when</u>, <u>where</u>, or <u>why</u> words comes before the subject, it is usually followed by a comma.

1   Try Out Your Skills

Vary each sentence by changing the order of the words.

> Because he was late, José missed half the movie.
> José missed half the movie because he was late.

1. During my lunch hour, I shared a pizza with Dave.

   _____

2. The President explained his policies at a news conference.

   _____

3. I didn't understand the instructions until you explained them.

   _____

4. In the summer, we often take our children to the pool.

   _____

5. Please clean the living room if you're staying home.

   _____

6. At the supermarket, I bought pork, rice, and beans.

   _____

7. Let's meet for dinner on Friday.

   _____

8. In fifteen minutes, I'll be ready to leave.

   _____

9. Please give me a call before you leave.

   _____

10. I walked to work because I missed the bus.

    _____

☐ **Check your answers on page 81.**

2 Try Out Your Skills

In the following story, all the sentences follow the same pattern. Rewrite the story. Change the pattern of the underlined sentences to provide variety.

> Sam goes camping in the mountains every summer. His children went with him last summer. The children were excited about the trip at first. They looked forward to sleeping outdoors. Their excitement didn't last long, though. They were unhappy when they saw that camping was hard work. They didn't like carrying heavy packs in the heat. They had to do a lot of chores after they reached the campsite. They wanted to go home and watch TV instead. They felt a little better after a good meal. Then Sam told them stories. Sam's children were good campers after a few days.

Every summer, Sam goes camping in the mountains.

_____

_____

_____

_____

_____

_____

_____

_____

_____

_____

☐ **Check your answers on page 81.**

3 Use Your Skills

In this passage, underline five sentences that could be varied to be more interesting. Then rewrite the passage with the varied sentence patterns.

I take a week off from work every year. I like to take my vacation during the fall. I usually drive north to New England in early October. I love watching the leaves turn to bright shades of red, yellow, and orange. The weather is usually beautiful at that time of year. It's cool, crisp, and sunny. I go for long walks and visit the apple orchards. You can pick your own fruit at some of them.

I usually stay with my friends Pete and Kathy in Massachusetts. We cook outdoors in the evening when the weather isn't too cold. We sit near the fireplace and talk on cold nights. It's good to see old friends no matter what the weather is like.

Every year, I take a week off from work.

_____

_____

_____

_____

_____

_____

_____

_____

_____

☐ **Check your answers on page 81.**

4   Use Your Skills

For each sentence, write a related sentence that follows a different pattern.

> I took driving lessons for two weeks.
> Last week, I got my driver's license.

1. During the summer, I dieted and worked out.

_____

2. I want to spend my vacation at home this year.

_____

3. In the spring, the baseball season starts.

_____

4. We finished dinner at seven o'clock.

_____

5. Luis usually eats spicy foods at restaurants.

_____

6. If it's sunny, I don't want to stay home.

_____

7. In the park, Donna gets a lot of exercise.

_____

8. The children did all their chores in the morning.

_____

9. At the end of the month, I paid all my bills.

_____

10. In September, Eric and Sue got engaged.

_____

☐ **Check your answers on page 81.**

5 Sum It Up

Complete these sentences about what you learned in Chapter 7.
Then check your answers on page 81. If you need more practice,
you can re-read the beginning of the chapter and repeat any of
the exercises.

Sentences can be ＿＿＿＿＿＿ by changing the ＿＿＿＿＿＿

of words. If all your sentences followed the same

＿＿＿＿＿＿, your writing would be ＿＿＿＿＿.

In Your Own Words

Write six or more related sentences about what you do on a typical
weekday. Each sentence should follow a different pattern from the
one before it. Here is how someone might begin:

At seven o'clock, I get up and turn on the news. I . . .

＿＿＿＿＿＿＿＿＿＿＿＿＿＿＿＿＿＿＿＿＿＿＿＿＿＿＿＿

＿＿＿＿＿＿＿＿＿＿＿＿＿＿＿＿＿＿＿＿＿＿＿＿＿＿＿＿

＿＿＿＿＿＿＿＿＿＿＿＿＿＿＿＿＿＿＿＿＿＿＿＿＿＿＿＿

＿＿＿＿＿＿＿＿＿＿＿＿＿＿＿＿＿＿＿＿＿＿＿＿＿＿＿＿

＿＿＿＿＿＿＿＿＿＿＿＿＿＿＿＿＿＿＿＿＿＿＿＿＿＿＿＿

＿＿＿＿＿＿＿＿＿＿＿＿＿＿＿＿＿＿＿＿＿＿＿＿＿＿＿＿

＿＿＿＿＿＿＿＿＿＿＿＿＿＿＿＿＿＿＿＿＿＿＿＿＿＿＿＿

＿＿＿＿＿＿＿＿＿＿＿＿＿＿＿＿＿＿＿＿＿＿＿＿＿＿＿＿

＿＿＿＿＿＿＿＿＿＿＿＿＿＿＿＿＿＿＿＿＿＿＿＿＿＿＿＿

＿＿＿＿＿＿＿＿＿＿＿＿＿＿＿＿＿＿＿＿＿＿＿＿＿＿＿＿

☐ **A sample is on page 81.**

CHAPTER 8

Sentence Combining

A painter can create a variety of effects by combining colors and shapes in different ways. A writer can do the same by using different combinations of words and sentences.

Sentence combining improves sentences by eliminating unnecessary words and by joining related ideas. The result is a better writing style—one that says more with fewer words.

> ■ **REMEMBER:** Sentence combining can make two or more related sentences into one sentence by choosing the necessary elements from the original sentences.

FOCUS ON SENTENCE SKILLS

Contrast the first two sentences with the third:

> John bought a car. The car is an old blue Ford.
> John bought an old blue Ford.

The second sentence repeats information given in the first sentence. That information, the car, can be eliminated when the sentences are combined. The verb is was dropped as well, since the combined sentence uses the verb that is related to John, the subject of the new sentence.

Sentences can be combined in many ways. Look carefully at the following examples to see how different combinations work:

> The new pitcher is talented. He won sixteen games last season.
> The talented new pitcher won sixteen games last season.

Tina is smart. Mike is smart too.
Tina and Mike are smart.

Julio is a good cook. He likes to try new recipes.
Julio is a good cook who likes to try new recipes.

Friday is a work day. Saturday isn't a work day.
Friday is a work day, but Saturday isn't.

We're going to the park. It's nice and quiet there.
We're going to the park, where it's nice and quiet.

I'm going to the store. I have to buy butter. I have to buy milk. I also need bread.
I'm going to the store to buy butter, milk, and bread.

Dolores practiced the guitar every day. She became a good guitarist.
Because Dolores practiced the guitar every day, she became a good guitarist.

As you can see from the last example, not all sentence pairs become shorter when they are combined. However, they do become clearer and more interesting.

1   Try Out Your Skills

Combine these pairs of sentences. You can add, remove, or change the order of words.

Last night I watched a movie. It was fascinating.
Last night I watched a fascinating movie.

1. You should dress warmly. It's getting very cold.

   _____

2. Carla came to the party. Rick didn't come to the party.

   _____

3. I'm taking some time off in July. It will be warmer then.

   _____

4. I put the children to bed. They were tired.

   _____

5. Sandra goes to school at night. Connie goes to school at night, too.

_____

6. I'd like some sugar in my coffee. I'd also like some milk.

_____

7. The thief was charged as a juvenile. She was young.

_____

8. Jack is a good friend. He always helps me.

_____

9. I'll call you before I leave. I'm going to leave this evening.

_____

10. We're going to the factory. Greg works there.

_____

☐ **Check your answers on page 81.**

2 Try Out Your Skills

Combine each set of sentences into one longer sentence.

> Frank bought a blouse. It was dark blue. He bought it for his wife.
> Frank bought a dark blue blouse for his wife.

1. Linda made a great dish. It was spicy. It had seafood in it.

_____

2. I have to do the laundry. I also have to make the beds. I have to clean the living room, too.

_____

3. Bob received a letter. It came from Miami. It was from his parents.

_____

4. We're going to the station. We're meeting my brother there. We're meeting him at nine o'clock.

_____

5. Ken is a good typist. Laura is a good typist. Ed is a good typist, too.

_____

6. I'm sending a package to my sister. She lives in Colombia. There are some books and magazines in the package.

_____

7. Let's go the beach. We can go when the weather clears. Let's take the train there.

_____

8. Jeff is a hard worker. He works in the sales department. He works ten hours a day.

_____

9. The weather was terrible. We didn't have a picnic. We didn't play ball, either.

_____

10. I'm going to wear the red sweater. It's warm. My sister made it for me.

_____

☐ **Check your answers on page 82.**

3   Use Your Skills

Combine each numbered sentence with a related lettered sentence. Then write your new sentences on the next page.

f	1. I like to go for walks in the evening.	**a.** The call was from my boss.
_____	2. I was too tired to go out.	**b.** It's warmer there.
_____	3. I was interrupted by a phone call.	**c.** My wife was too tired to go out last night.
_____	4. I have to buy a birthday gift.	**d.** Let's remember to do it before we leave.
_____	5. I like my new job.	**e.** My friends didn't show up at the party.
_____	6. Let's sit in the sun.	**f.** The weather is cooler then.
_____	7. I don't like most desserts.	**g.** I won't do it until everyone gets here.
_____	8. Let's close all the windows.	**h.** I don't like all the overtime.
_____	9. I was disappointed.	**i.** I love ice cream.
_____	10. I'm not going to serve dinner yet.	**j.** I need a birthday card, too.

1. **I like to go for walks in the evening, when the weather is cooler.**

2. _____

_____

3. _____

_____

4. _____

_____

5. _____

_____

6. _____

_____

7. _____

_____

8. _____

_____

9. _____

_____

10. _____

_____

☐ **Check your answers on page 82.**

4   Use Your Skills

Combine these related sentences. You can add or remove words as necessary.

Gloria is taking courses. She takes them at night. The courses are given at a business school. The school is downtown. She studies hard. She wants a better job. Gloria is going to write a new résumé. She'll write it in the summer. She doesn't have much work experience. She can write about the courses she's taking. She'll also get recommendations. She'll get them from her teachers. The recommendations will probably be excellent. Gloria is such a good student.

Gloria will go to employment agencies. She'll answer ads in the newspaper, too. She'll do it in September. She hopes she'll get an interesting job. She wants one by the end of the fall.

Gloria is taking courses at night

_____

_____

_____

_____

_____

_____

_____

_____

_____

☐ **Check your answers on page 82.**

5 Sum It Up

Complete these sentences about what you learned in Chapter 8. Then check your answers on page 82. If you need more practice, you can re-read the beginning of the chapter and repeat any of the exercises.

In sentence _____, two or more _____

sentences can be made into one. You can improve sentences by

_____ unnecessary words and by _____ re-

lated ideas.

In Your Own Words

Write at least five related sentences about something you would like to study. Each sentence should have enough information to form more than one simple sentence. Here is how someone might begin:

If I had some free time, I would study painting at an art school. . . .

_____

_____

_____

_____

_____

_____

_____

_____

☐ **A sample is on page 82.**

CHAPTER 9

Sentence Reduction

Most people are concerned with keeping their bodies fit and trim. It's also important to keep sentences fit and trim. This can be done by using **sentence reduction** to cut out excess words.

■ **REMEMBER:** In sentence reduction, all excess words are removed from a sentence.

FOCUS ON SENTENCE SKILLS

Compare these sentences:

My sister Sue, she's in the kitchen cooking dinner in the kitchen.
My sister Sue is in the kitchen cooking dinner.

In the first sentence, she repeats the subject, Sue, and in the kitchen is used twice. In the reduced sentence, these repeated parts are eliminated.

When you look for excess words, watch for the following:

1. words that mean the same thing in the same sentence

a true fact

2. phrases that repeat an idea in different parts of a sentence

In the summer, I like to go to the beach in the summer.

3. identifying a person or an object twice

Sara, she . . .   The dog, it . . .

1 Try Out Your Skills

In each sentence, underline the words that repeat the same thought. Then rewrite the sentence, leaving out the repeated words.

Since Eva didn't hear <u>the question</u>, she couldn't give an answer to <u>the question</u>.

Since Eva didn't hear the question, she couldn't give an answer.

1. Those Belindo children, they are making too much noise.

_____

2. Your answer is wrong and incorrect.

_____

3. Lisa and Carlos, they're coming to dinner tomorrow.

_____

4. I liked your shirt so much that I bought an identical, same one.

_____

5. The shouting fans shouted their favorite player's name.

_____

6. Do you like this small, little TV?

_____

7. After falling to the ground, the boy got up from the ground.

_____

8. Mr. Ito cleaned the cut on his son's cut knee.

_____

9. When Gordy checked his wallet, he found he had no money in his wallet.

_____

10. My father, he visited us last month.

_____

☐ **Check your answers on page 82.**

2 Try Out Your Skills

Reduce each sentence to as few words as possible without changing its meaning.

> The rain began to fall so steadily in a continuous downpour that the ball game was postponed because of the weather.
>
> The rain began to fall so steadily that the ball game was postponed.

1. Early in the morning at seven o'clock A.M., the ocean seemed calm and peaceful to the people who were resting and relaxing on the beach.

_____

2. The police chief, he sent out a group or party of people to search the nearby wooded forest.

_____

3. The sleepy, tired jurors, exhausted from the long trial that had lasted several weeks, they filed back into the courtroom of the courthouse.

_____

4. The national President of the United States will greet and shake hands with the returning astronauts who have come back from outer space.

_____

5. Last night, before today, we watched a dull, boring TV program on our new TV set that we bought recently.

_____

6. We sometimes occasionally pack our picnic basket with a picnic and drive in the car to a nearby park a few miles away.

_____

7. In April, in the spring, we always clean the apartment and paint the apartment every year.

_____

8. My daughter, she has a large record collection of a lot of records.

_____

9. My favorite old movie, which I like the most, is <u>Gone with the Wind</u>, a movie made a long time ago.

_____

10. Gary's used motorcycle, which isn't new, was inexpensive and didn't cost much money.

_____

☐ **Check your answers on page 82.**

3 Use Your Skills

Rewrite these related sentences. Reduce each sentence to eliminate related thoughts.

Since yesterday was wet and rainy, we couldn't go to the park to play ball in the park. The weather was so terrible and awful out that we couldn't go outside because of the weather. We had to stay in our small, tiny apartment all day, from morning until night. We tried calling our friends on the telephone, but no one answered the phone. Then we watched some dull TV, which was really boring to watch. We ended up eating and devouring all the food in the refrigerator. Rainy days aren't much fun, and they aren't a pleasure, either.

Since yesterday was rainy, _____

_____

_____

_____

_____

_____

_____

☐ **Check your answers on page 82.**

4   Use Your Skills

Reduce these sentences as much as possible.

Last month, just one month ago, my parents flew here on a plane for a short three-day visit. I hadn't seen them in almost a year, or twelve months. We were all of us happy and pleased to see each other. My parents, they had lots of gifts and presents for the children. My mother brought homemade bread that she made at home. She is always afraid all the time that I don't eat enough. My father took a lot of color pictures and photos using color film. It was great and wonderful to see my parents again, but their visits are always exhausting and tiring. I think I'll go to their home to visit them next time.

Last month, my parents flew here
_____

_____

_____

_____

_____

_____

_____

_____

_____

_____

_____

☐ **Check your answers on page 83.**

5 Sum It Up

Complete these sentences about what you learned in Chapter 9. Then check your answers on page 83. If you need more practice, you can re-read the chapter and repeat any of the exercises.

In sentence _____, all excess words are _____

from a sentence. In sentences, you should always watch out for

words that mean the _____ thing, for identifying a

_____ or an _____ twice, and for phrases that

_____ an idea in different places.

In Your Own Words

Write six or more related sentences about something unusual that happened to you. As you write, think about keeping your sentences trim. When you are finished, re-read the sentences to make sure there are no excess words. Here is how someone might begin:

Last summer, I had a very unusual experience. . . .

_____

_____

_____

_____

_____

_____

_____

_____

_____

_____

☐ **A sample is on page 83.**

CHAPTER 10

The Topic Sentence

The groups of related sentences you have been writing are paragraphs. The **topic sentence** is the most important sentence in a paragraph. It tells the reader what idea you are going to develop. For example, if your topic is "Surviving a Divorce," your topic sentence might be, "I learned some important lessons from my divorce." Another topic sentence might be "Getting divorced isn't the end of the world." In both cases, you have stated an idea that can be developed into a paragraph.

A topic sentence is usually the first or last sentence in a paragraph, since it either introduces or summarizes the idea of that paragraph.

■ **REMEMBER:** The topic sentence is the main sentence in a paragraph. It states the idea that the paragraph develops.

FOCUS ON SENTENCE SKILLS

To write a topic sentence, you must:

1. understand your topic;
2. have an idea you wish to state about the topic; and
3. state the idea in sentence form.

In developing a topic sentence, you can use this outline:

  I. Topic (word or words)
  II. Idea About Topic (phrase or brief sentence)
  III. Topic Sentence (complete sentence expressing the main idea of the paragraph)

1 Try Out Your Skills

Write a brief, general idea for each topic.

> **Family Budgets**
> Families should use a budget to help them handle money.

1. Television Today

   _____

2. My Neighborhood

   _____

3. My Favorite Restaurant

   _____

4. If I Won the Lottery

   _____

5. My Most Important Decision

   _____

6. Someone I'd Like to Meet

   _____

7. Raising Healthy Children

   _____

8. What's Important in a Friendship

   _____

9. Learning from Experience

   _____

10. Moving to a New City

   _____

☐ **Check your answers on page 83.**

2 Try Out Your Skills

For each topic and general idea in Exercise 1, write a complete, specific topic sentence.

1. **Families will be able to save more money if they use a budget to keep track of income and expenses.**

2. _____

_____

3. _____

_____

4. _____

_____

5. _____

_____

6. _____

_____

7. _____

_____

8. _____

_____

9. _____

_____

10. _____

_____

☐ **Check your answers on page 83.**

3   Use Your Skills

You can develop many different topic sentences for any given topic. Create two topic sentences for each of these topics.

> Spending Your Free Time
> **a.** There are many different ways to spend your free time. _____
> **b.** Free time is usually in short supply, so use it wisely. _____

1. Preparing for an Interview

   a. _____

   b. _____

2. Smoking in Public Places

   a. _____

   b. _____

3. Kids Today

   a. _____

   b. _____

4. Solving Family Problems

   a. _____

   b. _____

5. Why Men and Women Fight

   a. _____

   b. _____

6. Do Diets Work?

   a. _____

   b. _____

7. Violence on TV

    a. _____

    b. _____

8. How Women's Roles Are Changing

    a. _____

    b. _____

9. My Greatest Challenge

    a. _____

    b. _____

10. Getting Along with a Boss

    a. _____

    b. _____

☐ **Check your answers on page 83.**

4 Use Your Skills

Write a topic sentence for each paragraph.

> It is important for husbands and wives to share housework. Today, in many families, both the husband and wife work outside the home. As a result, they are both equally tired at the end of the day and at the end of the week. Housework can pile up and soon become more than one person can handle. This may lead to arguments between the husband and wife .

1. _____

   Criminal lawyers defend or prosecute people accused of committing crimes. Corporate lawyers work for big businesses or corporations. Other lawyers work in the areas of civil rights, family court, and legal aid for the poor.

2. _____

   It is used to season food. It can also be used as a preservative, helping to keep food from spoiling. Salt pills are sometimes used to help a person's body get rid of water.

3. _____

   It requires stamina and speed. Tennis players must be alert on the court at all times. They also need a good eye and a good sense of distance and timing.

4. _____

   If you don't dress properly, you probably won't get the job. Your appearance may be as important as your résumé. It indicates to an employer how serious you are about your work.

5. _____

   Caring for them can help teach children responsibility. They are good company for older people whose spouses have died. Some pets, like large dogs, can provide protection. Dogs are also good for lazy people; walking them is great exercise.

☐ **Check your answers on page 83.**

5 Sum It Up

Complete these sentences about what you learned in Chapter 10. Then check your answers on page 83. If you need more practice, you can re-read the beginning of the chapter and repeat any of the exercises.

The _____ sentence is the most important sentence in

a paragraph. It indicates the _____ you are going to

develop. It is usually the _____ or _____

sentence of a paragraph.

In Your Own Words

Write a paragraph of five or more related sentences on the topic "My Advice to Parents Today." Be sure you have a strong topic sentence. Here is how someone might begin:

Because children are growing up in a world of problems, they need guidance . . . .

_____

_____

_____

_____

_____

_____

_____

_____

_____

☐ **A sample is on page 84.**

POST-TEST

1 Begin or end each sentence by completing the thought.

  1. When will _____?

  2. _____ during the winter.

  3. Don't _____!

  4. Can you _____?

  5. _____ are fascinating places.

2 Draw a line below the simple subject in each sentence. Then draw two lines below the simple verb.

  6. Rick's old car needs a lot of repairs.

  7. Do you like your new apartment?

  8. I was called for jury duty last week.

  9. Where are your parents moving?

  10. Our children study very hard.

3 Change each fragment to a sentence. Add words to the beginning or end of the fragment to complete the thought.

  11. When the home team scored.

  _____

  12. If you're not too busy.

  _____

  13. Because Pamela is deaf.

  _____

14. Before I leave the office.

   _____

15. Every Sunday morning at eleven o'clock.

   _____

4 Rewrite each run-on sentence as two or more correct sentences.

16. We're leaving at eight o'clock, will you be ready then?

   _____

17. Jim bought some lettuce and he bought some tomatoes and he also bought some onions.

   _____

18. Let's go out it's too hot in here.

   _____

   _____

19. Pablo likes to go dancing Anita prefers to stay home.

   _____

   _____

20. The children are upstairs, they're fast asleep.

   _____

   _____

5 Replace the general word in each sentence with a more specific one.

21. I love to read <u>books</u>. _____

22. Our neighbors are very <u>nice</u>. _____

23. If the weather is <u>good</u>, we can go to the beach. _____

24. Let's plant some <u>flowers</u> in the windowbox. _____

25. Ms. Wong <u>said</u>, "You must fill out this form." _____

6 Rewrite each sentence so that it answers the questions in parentheses.

26. I made a doctor's appointment. (when, why)

_____

_____

27. Bill and Jenny are taking a vacation. (where, when)

_____

_____

28. We're catching a train. (where, when)

_____

_____

29. Sara stopped smoking. (when, why)

_____

_____

30. Don rode his bicycle. (where, why)

_____

_____

7 Vary each sentence by changing the order of the words.

31. Every morning at seven o'clock, I listen to the news.

_____

32. At the train station, Anna ran into an old friend.

_____

33. The weather in the city is terrible during the summer.

_____

34. Because of the rain, we had to cancel the game.

_____

35. We were very nervous until the guests arrived.

_____

8 Combine each set of sentences into one longer sentence.

36. Barbara bought a used car. The car is beautiful.

_____

37. We arrived on time. Our friends didn't arrive on time.

_____

38. I like to go hiking. I do it in the fall.

_____

39. Let's pack our bathing suits. We might pass a lake.

_____

40. Bob made a salad. He used lettuce. He used tomatoes. He also used carrots.

_____

_____

9 In each sentence, underline the words that repeat the same thought. Then rewrite the sentence, leaving out the repeated words.

41. My friend Jim, he just got married.

_____

42. Maria is at the office finishing work at the office.

_____

43. Tom told a dishonest lie on his job application.

_____

44. We stayed up late last night until midnight.

_____

45. Your brothers, are they coming to the wedding?

_____

10 **46.–50.** In many families today, both the husband and wife work full time. What might this mean to the children in the family? Write a paragraph of at least five sentences on this topic. Be sure that you have a strong topic sentence.

Children of Working Couples

_____

_____

_____

_____

_____

_____

_____

_____

_____

_____

_____

_____

_____

☐ **Check your answers on page 84.**

Post-Test Evaluation Chart

Use the Answer Key to check your answers. Circle the number of any item you missed. The chart will show you which chapters you may want to review further.

Exercise	Item					Chapter
1	1	2	3	4	5	1
2	6	7	8	9	10	2
3	11	12	13	14	15	3
4	16	17	18	19	20	4
5	21	22	23	24	25	5
6	26	27	28	29	30	6
7	31	32	33	34	35	7
8	36	37	38	39	40	8
9	41	42	43	44	45	9
10	46–50					10

PRE-TEST

1 (sample answers)

1. is on the third floor   2. Do you want   3. Aunt Lucy and I   4. looking for a new apartment   5. are exciting sports

2 (sample answers)

1. The children ran home from school.   2. My brother plays the guitar.   3. Are your friends driving you home?   4. This movie is very scary!   5. We watched the papers for a sale.

3 11. (c)   12. (e)   13. (a)   14. (b)   15. (d)

4 16. I got up early. I had a lot to do. Right after breakfast, I made a list of all my chores. 17. Jack went to the movies. Did Tina go, too?   18. We went to the park. We had a picnic. Then we played ball.   19. I'm tired. Let's stay home and watch TV.   20. It's getting late. You're going to miss the bus.

5 (sample answers)

21. hamburger   22. comfortable   23. cried   24. stormy   25. station wagon

6 (sample answers)

26. I'm going to Chicago to visit my friend.   27. The children went to bed at eight o'clock.   28. Maria didn't come with us because she had to work late.   29. I will look for a second job in May.   30. I parked the car six blocks away.

7 31. In the winter, I like to go ice skating.   32. We met Rick and Pauline at the party. 33. During the movie, the children ate three boxes of raisins.   34. You shouldn't walk home alone because it's getting dark.   35. When you called, I was cleaning the apartment.

8 (sample answers)

36. I bought a warm coat last winter.   37. Don and I are going to the union meeting. 38. Let's take an umbrella because it might rain.   39. I want to move, but Bill doesn't. 40. We had eggs and toast for breakfast.

9 (sample answers)

41. (Ken, he) My friend Ken goes to school at night.   42. (tiny, little) Sara uses a tiny adding machine at work.   43. (to the store ... at the store) We went to the store and bought groceries.   44. (right and correct) Your answer was right.   45. (Late at night ... eleven P.M.) At eleven P.M., we usually watch the news.

10 (sample answers)

46. Every company should provide day-care facilities for the children of its employees. 47. Patience is the key to getting along with neighbors.   48. The most important office rules are the ones that the employees' handbook never mentions.   49. It took a family gathering to make me really appreciate my grandparents.   50. Women are still fighting the battle of "equal pay for equal work."

CHAPTER 1

1 1. The new museum has modern paintings.   2. Seven people were waiting in the rain for the bus.   3. I won $5,000 in the state lottery!   4. Can you come to work earlier tomorrow?   5. Last night we watched a great movie on TV.   6. Do your children like spicy food?   7. In the spring, Maria will join a softball team.   8. My typewriter needs a new ribbon.   9. Have Ken and Yoko found a new apartment yet?   10. Millions of people cross this bridge every day.

2 1. (c) 2. (g) 3. (j) 4. (a) 5. (b) 6. (d) 7. (i) 8. (e) 9. (f) 10. (h)

3 (sample answers)

1. turned on his headlights.   2. I like to go to football games.   3. borrow this book?   4. has a view of the river.   5. went very well.   6. I started my new job.   7. make a lot of noise?   8. is very small.   9. I usually take a coffee break.   10. offer you that promotion?

4 (sample answers)

1. Do your children   2. The mayor   3. Skiing and ice skating   4. Architects   5. Were you   6. News of the robbery   7. Professional athletes   8. That movie   9. Are your friends   10. Your new ring

5 sentence; complete subject; complete verb

In Your Own Words (sample answer)

My neighbor Anita is a very unusual person. She works as a word processor during the day and goes to school five nights a week. At school, she takes courses in hotel management. Anita wants to run her own hotel some day. She'll probably succeed because she has a lot of talent and determination.

CHAPTER 2

1 1. Our new neighbors moved in yesterday.   2. That red tie looks awful with your yellow shirt!   3. What did the crying child want?   4. My two favorite foods are pizza and chili.   5. Last night my best friend called from California.   6. Barbara's fat cat ate all her plants!   7. The cold, stormy weather kept us indoors all day.   8. A strange letter arrived in the mail this morning.   9. Are the people on this list coming to the party?   10. The long, boring game lasted until midnight.

2 1. I always walk very quickly.   2. Do you watch the news at night?   3. Mario won the game with his home run.   4. Every weekend Leroy drives a cab.   5. Lisa drove carefully because of the rain.   6. My brother wrote an angry letter to the newspaper.   7. Are both of the children sleeping?   8. Our phone rang late last night.   9. Mrs. Gomez worries about her son.   10. Did you get a raise this year?

3 (sample answers)

1. My sister works at an auto plant.   2. My friends liked the gift I brought them.   3. My family is visiting us this week.   4. The children watch too much TV.   5. The restaurant was a real treat.   6. Do you like Japanese food?   7. What does your son want for his birthday?   8. Did those people see the accident?   9. Can that pitcher throw fastballs?   10. Why are the workers complaining?

4 (sample answers)

1. (g) This Mexican food needs more spice!   2. (a) That movie bored me to tears.   3. (b) Linda's apartment is tiny.   4. (d) This book seems interesting.   5. (j) Ruby's voice shook over the phone.   6. (c) My parents called last night.   7. (h) My friends saw the play last week.   8. (f) Most children like ice cream.   9. (e) That man bought another ticket.   10. (i) Our team played well yesterday.

5 key; simple; simple verb; basic

In Your Own Words (sample answer)

In my free time, I watch sports on TV. My favorite sport is football. I like its fast pace and excitement. Sometimes my husband and I invite friends over for the important games. Then our living room sounds like a football stadium!

CHAPTER 3

1   1. (d)   2. (j)   3. (i)   4. (a)   5. (g)   6. (h)   7. (f)   8. (e)   9. (c)   10. (b)

2   (fragments)

When seven o'clock comes. If my children didn't shout to wake me up. Unless my oldest daughter is dieting. Even though she is already thin. After we finish breakfast. Even though some mornings I would rather go back to bed!

3   (sample answers)

1. Whenever you have time, please take a look at this.   2. We went for a walk after the rain stopped.   3. When the day ends, I must relax.   4. Mae moved in with her son after her husband died.   5. If you want to help me, you can slice the vegetables.   6. Although the weather doesn't look good, we're playing ball.   7. We went out for coffee when the movie ended.   8. Since the office closes at five o'clock, I cannot finish this today.   9. I checked my notes before the tenants' meeting began.   10. Because it's dark out, you should take a flashlight.

4   When our hopes were almost gone, our company softball team won the big game. Since we had been the underdogs, we were all overjoyed. Before the game began, we were nervous and unsure of ourselves. Because we had good teamwork, we were able to play better than ever before. Now it was over, and we had won. Although it hadn't always seemed that way, all our hard practice had been worthwhile.

5   incomplete; complete; add; join; sentence

In Your Own Words   (sample answer)

When the weather on the weekend is terrible, we usually have to change our plans. Since we can't go out, we find interesting things to do indoors. If we can't find any chores to do, we usually end up reading or listening to music. As dinnertime approaches, we often prepare a big meal together. Then we play cards if it's still raining. Before we go to bed, we watch a movie on TV. If we can find interesting things to do indoors, rainy days aren't so bad.

CHAPTER 4

1   (run-ons)

1. (3)   4. (3)   5. (2)   6. (2)   7. (2)   9. (3)

2   My interview was very tiring, it took almost an hour and the manager's assistant tested my typing and I was very nervous and I made some mistakes, I didn't do very well I probably won't get the job but at least I tried my best, I have another interview tomorrow, I really want the job I'll do better after a good night's sleep.

3   1. Elena was late. They started the meeting without her.   2. Bill had so much work to do! He had to do the laundry. He had to go shopping. Then he had to make dinner.   3. Claudia made a mistake. She tried to hide it. She got caught.   4. Julio found a wallet in the street. He looked inside it for identification. He found a driver's license and some credit cards.   5. The children are tired. Put them to bed.   6. We went to the store. First we bought food for the party. Then we bought cups and napkins.   7. My son is almost five. His birthday is next week.   8. Our union may call a strike. I am very worried.   9. We're leaving soon. Why don't you come with us?   10. Gloria looks sad. She probably didn't get the job.

4   (sample answers)

1. It's getting late, so we should leave soon.   2. Call me early in the morning because my train leaves at eight o'clock.   3. Although the prices are getting lower, they're still high.   4. I'd like to see that movie, so tell me if you decide to go.   5. Since it's your birthday, I'd like to take you out to dinner.   6. We canceled our trip because the car broke down.   7. I'm tired, so let's finish the project in the morning.   8. Dress warmly because it gets cold here at night.   9. Since the bus is late, I'll be late for work.   10. Don't give candy to the children because it's not good for them.

5   run-on; written; punctuation; comma; sentence; ands

In Your Own Words   (sample answer)

Being a good employee means more than just doing good work. It also means having a good work attitude. Getting along well with other employees is also very important because people must work together. They have to respect one another. Although you might not like all your co-workers, you must co-operate with them. If you are very unhappy about your job situation, you should think it over. Perhaps you are not working at a job that is right for you.

CHAPTER 5

1 (sample answers)
1. roses   2. golden retriever   3. supermarket   4. Volkswagen   5. bee   6. pineapple   7. rock   8. pepper   9. ocean   10. necklace

2 (sample answers)
1. a. kind   b. friendly   2. a. fascinating   b. thrilling   3. a. sunny   b. pleasant   4. a. rainy   b. cold   5. a. accurate   b. careful

3 (sample answer)
Last night, I was watching an <u>exciting</u> movie on TV when the phone rang. It was my old friend, Rita.

"What a <u>wonderful</u> surprise!" I <u>exclaimed</u>. "I haven't heard from you in <u>six months</u>!"

"That's because I moved <u>in September</u>," <u>explained</u> Rita. "I got a <u>well-paying</u> job as a <u>computer programmer</u> in Chicago. I also found a <u>roomy</u> apartment outside the city. It has a <u>beautiful</u> backyard with a garden. Last week, I planted <u>tulips</u> and <u>lettuce</u>!"

"That sounds <u>fabulous</u>!" I <u>commented</u>. "I can't wait to visit you!"

4 (sample answer)
Last year, Mike and Sue were in a <u>serious</u> car accident. Their car ended up <u>demolished</u>. They saved their money for <u>eight months</u> to buy another car. They were <u>overjoyed</u> when they found a used one. It's <u>seven years</u> old, but it's <u>in excellent condition</u>. It has a lot of <u>practical</u> features, and it's <u>comfortable</u> to drive. Sue doesn't like the color, though. The car is <u>tan</u>, and she wants to paint it <u>black</u>.

5 general; specific; confusing; dull

In Your Own Words (sample answer)
<u>Star Wars</u> is the fastest-paced, most exciting movie ever made. Its special effects are spectacular. The movie's young producer, George Lucas, is one of the most talented filmmakers of our time. The entire cast is superb, too. <u>Star Wars</u> was first shown in 1977, but its power will stand the test of time.

CHAPTER 6

1 1. who, what, when, why   2. who, what, where   3. who, what, where   4. who, what, where, when   5. who, what, when   6. who what, when   7. who, what, where   8. who, what, where, when   9. who, what   10. who, what, where

2 (sample answers)
1. Marta ate a big breakfast <u>at the diner</u> this morning because she was very hungry.   2. Bob wore a clean blue shirt to work <u>yesterday</u>.   3. The children are swimming at the school gym <u>right now</u>.   4. Last night we had dinner at the pizzeria <u>because we didn't have time to cook</u>.   5. Dwight struck out eleven batters <u>at Shea Stadium</u> yesterday.   6. Sue has an interview <u>at the telephone company</u> at eleven o'clock.   7. Kahlil is doing the wash at the laundromat <u>this morning</u>.   8. Tomorrow we're going to the concert in the park <u>because the program looks really exciting</u>.   9. Bill couldn't get tickets for the baseball game <u>because they were sold out in advance</u>.   10. Seventeen people are going to the party at Paula's apartment <u>on Saturday</u>.

3 (sample answers)
1. We're taking the bus <u>to the department store</u>.   2. Kim left work early <u>on Friday</u>.   3. <u>In the spring</u>, I'd like to take a trip.   4. Carla doesn't want to be a secretary <u>because she hates to type</u>.   5. Frank and Luis went shopping <u>downtown</u>.   6. I hate department stores <u>because they're so crowded</u>.   7. My friend just started a new job <u>in Philadelphia</u>.   8. We finished all our work <u>at five o'clock</u>.   9. I need some new clothes <u>because I'm starting a new job</u>.   10. Let's have a picnic <u>in the park</u>.

4 (sample answers)
1. The children laughed <u>during the school play</u>. (who, what, when)   2. I decided to move <u>away from the city</u>. (who, what, where)   3. The game <u>last night</u> was exciting.

(who, what, when) 4. Ted invited ten guests to the party at his apartment. (who, what, where) 5. The apartment will be beautiful when we finish decorating it. (who, what, when) 6. We're taking the train because it's fast. (who, what, why) 7. Sam wrote to his brother in Texas. (who, what, where) 8. I'd like to go out because it's too hot in the apartment. (who, what, where, why) 9. My friends are visiting in June. (who, what, when) 10. I'm going to take a vacation in Canada next summer. (who, what, where, when)

5 expansion; who; what; where; when; why

In Your Own Words

(sample answer)

If I could have any job for just one day, I would be an astronaut. I'd like to travel to outer space because it would be exciting. Astronauts get to see unusual things far above the surface of the earth.

CHAPTER 7

1 1. I shared a pizza with Dave during my lunch hour. 2. At a news conference, the President explained his policies. 3. Until you explained them, I didn't understand the instructions. 4. We often take our children to the pool in the summer. 5. If you're staying home, please clean the living room. 6. I bought pork, rice, and beans at the supermarket. 7. On Friday, let's meet for dinner. 8. I'll be ready to leave in fifteen minutes. 9. Before you leave, please give me a call. 10. Because I missed the bus, I walked to work.

2 (revised sentences)

Every summer, Sam goes camping in the mountains. At first, the children were excited about the trip. When they saw that camping was hard work, they were unhappy. After they reached the campsite, they had to do a lot of chores. After a good meal, they felt a little better. After a few days, Sam's children were good campers.

3 (sample answer)

Every year, I take a week off from work. I like to take my vacation during the fall. In early October, I usually drive north to New England. I love watching the leaves turn to bright shades of red, yellow, and orange. At that time of year, the weather is usually beautiful. It's cool, crisp, and sunny. I go for long walks and visit the apple orchards. At some of them, you can pick your own fruit.

I usually stay with my friends Pete and Kathy in Massachusetts. When the weather isn't too cold, we cook outdoors in the evening. We sit near the fireplace and talk on cold nights. No matter what the weather is like, it's good to see old friends.

4 (sample answers)

1. I lost fifteen pounds by September. 2. Next year, I'd like to go away. 3. It doesn't end until October. 4. After dinner, we played cards. 5. At home, Luis eats hot dogs and hamburgers. 6. I want to go to the beach if the weather is good. 7. Donna just sits around at home. 8. In the afternoon, they went to the circus. 9. I don't owe anyone money for a while. 10. They will get married in April.

5 varied; position; pattern; dull

In Your Own Words

(sample answer)

At seven o'clock, I get up and turn on the news. I get dressed after I listen to the weather report. After breakfast, I leave for work. I answer phones and type letters until lunchtime. At noon, I usually eat with a friend at the company cafeteria. I leave the office at five o'clock. When I get home, I have dinner with my family. I usually read or watch TV until I go to bed.

CHAPTER 8

1 (sample answers)

1. You should dress warmly because it's getting very cold. 2. Carla came to the party, but Rick didn't. 3. I'm taking some time off in July, when the weather is warmer. 4. I put the children to bed because they were tired. 5. Sandra and Connie go to school at night. 6. I'd like some sugar and milk in my coffee. 7. The young thief was charged as a juvenile. 8. Jack is a good friend who always helps me out. 9. I'll call you before I leave this evening. 10. We're going to the factory where Greg works.

2 (sample answers)

1. Linda made a great spicy dish with vegetables and seafood.   2. I have to do the laundry, make the beds, and clean the living room.   3. Bob received a letter from his parents in Miami.   4. We're meeting my brother at the station at nine o'clock.   5. Ken, Linda, and Ed are good typists.   6. I'm sending a package of books and magazines to my sister in Colombia.   7. Let's take the train to the beach when the weather clears.   8. Jeff works hard in the sales department ten hours a day.   9. Because the weather was terrible, we didn't have a picnic or play ball.   10. I'm going to wear the warm red sweater that my sister made for me.

3 (sample answers)

1. (f) I like to go for walks in the evening, when the weather is cooler.   2. (c) We were too tired to go out last night.   3. (a) I was interrupted by a phone call from my boss.   4. (j) I have to buy a birthday gift and card.   5. (h) I like my new job, but I don't like all the overtime.   6. (b) Let's sit in the sun, where it's warmer.   7. (i) I don't like most desserts, but I love ice cream.   8. (d) Let's remember to close all the windows before we leave.   9. (e) I was disappointed when my friends didn't show up at the party.   10. (g) I'm not going to serve dinner until everyone gets here.

4 (sample answer)

Gloria is taking courses at night at a business school downtown. She studies hard because she wants a better job. Gloria is going to write a new résumé in the summer. She doesn't have much work experience, but she can write about the courses she's taking. She'll also get recommendations from her teachers. The recommendations will probably be excellent because Gloria is such a good student.

Gloria will go to employment agencies and answer ads in the newspaper in September. She hopes she'll get an interesting job by the end of the fall.

5 combining; related; eliminating; joining

In Your Own Words (sample answer)

If I had some free time, I would study painting at an art school. I love to draw, and my kids think my drawings are great. Because I draw well, I think I might paint well, too. I'd like to do portraits of my family and still lifes of things in the apartment. When the kids are all in school, I might have time for an art class.

CHAPTER 9

1 (sample answers)

1. (children, they) Those Belindo children are making too much noise.   2. (wrong, incorrect) Your answer is wrong.   3. (Lisa and Carlos, they) Lisa and Carlos are coming to dinner tomorrow.   4. (identical, same) I liked your shirt so much that I bought an identical one.   5. (shouting fans shouted) The fans shouted their favorite player's name.   6. (small, little) Do you like this little TV? 7. (to the ground . . . from the ground) After falling to the ground, the boy got up.   8. (cut . . . cut) Mr. Ito cleaned the cut on his son's knee.   9. (his wallet . . . in his wallet) When Gordy checked his wallet, he found he had no money.   10. (father, he) My father visited us last month.

2 (sample answers)

1. At seven o'clock in the morning, the ocean seemed calm to the people relaxing on the beach.   2. The police chief sent out a party to search the nearby forest.   3. The jurors, exhausted from the trial that had lasted several weeks, filed back into the courtroom.   4. The President of the United States will greet the returning astronauts.   5. Last night, we watched a boring program on our new TV set.   6. We sometimes pack our picnic basket and drive to a nearby park.   7. We clean and paint the apartment every April.   8. My daughter has a large record collection.   9. My favorite old movie is *Gone with the Wind.*   10. Gary's used motorcycle was inexpensive.

3 (sample answer)

Since yesterday was rainy, we couldn't go to the park to play ball. The weather was so terrible that we couldn't go outside. We had to stay in our tiny apartment all day. We tried calling friends, but no one answered. Then we watched some dull TV. We ended up eating all the food in the refrigerator. Rainy days aren't much fun.

4 (sample answer)

Last month, my parents flew here for a three-day visit. I hadn't seen them in almost a year. We were happy to see each other. My parents had lots of presents for the children. My mother brought homemade bread. She is always afraid that I don't eat enough. My father took a lot of color pictures. It was wonderful to see my parents again, but their visits are always exhausting. I think I'll visit them next time.

5 reduction; removed; same; person; object; repeat

In Your Own Words

(sample answer)

Last summer, I had a very unusual experience. I was on a fishing trip in Delaware with my family. We rented a small cabin near the river. Because the family next door was very friendly, we went fishing together. We had just met, but the man and I seemed very familiar to each other. After several days, I realized why. We had been in the same kindergarten class thirty years ago!

CHAPTER 10

1 (sample answers)

1. Television today is disappointing.   2. My neighborhood is changing for the better.   3. My favorite restaurant is very unusual.   4. If I won the lottery, I would handle the money wisely.   5. My most important decision was about my career.   6. I'd like to meet someone in politics.   7. Raising your children is the best thing you can do for them.   8. Friendship has several important characteristics.   9. Experience often has been called the best teacher.   10. Moving to a new city can be difficult.

2 (sample answers)

1. Television today is mostly for kids, who make up a big part of the viewing audience. 2. Our "Neighborhood Watch" program is making our block a safer place to live.   3. My favorite restaurant is one of the few small, family-run businesses left in town.   4. If I won the lottery, I would invest the money in my children's future.   5. My most important decision was to change careers after raising a family.   6. Geraldine Ferraro, candidate for Vice-President in the 1984 election, is someone I'd like to meet.   7. If you raise healthy children, they probably will become healthy adults.   8. The most important thing to me in a friend is dependability.   9. I have learned more from experience than I have from any book.   10. Moving to a new city is most difficult for children.

3 (sample answers)

1. a. Preparing for an interview is one of the most important steps in applying for a job. b. If you don't prepare for an interview, you might as well forget about the job.   2. a. Smoking in public places should be banned.   b. We need national restrictions on smoking in public places.   3. a. Kids today need more discipline.   b. It must be hard to be a kid today.   4. a. It's important to involve the whole family in solving family problems.   b. Solving family problems takes patience and understanding.   5. a. Men and women fight because of basic differences between the sexes.   b. Social pressures create most fights between men and women.   6. a. Diets don't work unless they change basic eating patterns.   b. People who go on diets usually gain back more weight than they lose.   7. a. Violence on TV can lead to violence in real life.   b. Violent programs should be restricted to late-night TV.   8. a. Women's roles are changing at work, at home, and in personal relationships.   b. As women are gaining more rights, their roles are changing. 9. a. When I was promoted to assistant department manager, I met my greatest challenge. b. My greatest challenge was getting to start in the biggest game of the season.   10. a. It takes patience and hard work to get along with a boss.   b. It's important, but often difficult, to get along with a boss.

4 (sample answers)

1. There are many different kinds of lawyers.   2. Salt is an important product with several uses.   3. Tennis is a very demanding sport.   4. Dressing for an interview is more important than most people think.   5. Pets are valuable for many kinds of people.

5 topic; idea; first; last

In Your Own Words   (sample answer)

Because children are growing up in a world of problems, they need guidance. They face more choices than ever before, and they need help in choosing wisely. Parents must be sensitive to children's special needs. They must be able to discuss issues like drugs and sex openly. Children should feel free to ask their parents questions about sensitive topics. In turn, parents must be well informed about these topics to help their children make responsible choices.

POST-TEST

1   (sample answers)

1. the train leave   2. I love to walk in the snow   3. stand so close to the edge   4. speak Spanish   5. Big cities

2   6. Rick's old <u>car</u> <u>needs</u> a lot of repairs.   7. <u>Do</u> <u>you</u> <u>like</u> your new apartment?   8. <u>I</u> <u>was</u> <u>called</u> for jury duty last week.   9. Where <u>are</u> your <u>parents</u> <u>moving</u>?   10. Our <u>children</u> <u>study</u> hard.

3   (sample answers)

11. <u>The crowd cheered</u> when the home team scored.   12. If you're not too busy, <u>please</u> <u>help me</u>.   13. Because Pamela is deaf, <u>she has learned to read lips</u>.   14. Before I leave the office, <u>I must make a phone call</u>.   15. <u>I go to church</u> every Sunday morning at eleven o'clock.

4   16. We're leaving at eight o'clock. Will you be ready then?   17. Jim bought some lettuce. He bought some tomatoes. He bought some onions.   18. Let's go out. It's too hot in here.   19. Pablo likes to go dancing. Anita prefers to stay home.   20. The children are upstairs. They're fast alseep.

5   (sample answers)

21. novels   22. friendly   23. sunny   24. tulips   25. explained

6   (sample answers)

26. I made a doctor's appointment <u>yesterday</u> because this cold won't go away.   27. <u>Next</u> <u>month</u>, Bill and Jenny are taking a vacation <u>in Florida</u>.   28. We're catching a train <u>to</u> <u>New York</u> at two o'clock.   29. Sara stopped smoking <u>last week</u> because she was <u>coughing</u> <u>all the time</u>.   30. Don rode his bicycle <u>to work</u> because he missed the bus.

7   31. I listen to the news every morning at seven o'clock.   32. Anna ran into an old friend at the train station.   33. During the summer, the weather in the city is terrible.   34. We had to cancel the game because of the rain.   35. Until the guests arrived, we were very nervous.

8   (sample answers)

36. Barbara bought a beautiful used car.   37. We arrived on time, but our friends didn't. 38. I like to go hiking in the fall.   39. Let's pack our bathing suits in case we pass a lake. 40. Bob used lettuce, tomatoes, and carrots in his salad.

9   (sample answers)

41. (Jim, he) My friend Jim just got married.   42. (at the office ... at the office) Maria is finishing work at the office.   43. (dishonest lie) Tom told a lie on his job application. 44. (late ... until midnight) We stayed up last night until midnight.   45. (Your brothers, are they) Are your brothers coming to the wedding?

10   (sample answer)

46.–50. When both husband and wife work, their children have to make many adjustments. They often have to come home from school to an empty house. As a result, they must be responsible for such things as starting their homework alone. Many such children often wind up with a greater share of housework. This, however, can be an advantage. They can clearly see that being a family is a "team effort," in which every member must be understanding and willing to do his or her share of the work. Making these adjustments can be difficult for some children. With loving help from their parents, however, it can be done.